LETTERS OF A COUNTRY POSTMAN

More Books by John B. Keane

Letters of a Successful T.D.

Letters of an Irish Parish Priest

Letters of a Love-Hungry Farmer

Letters of a Matchmaker

Letters of an Irish Publican

Letters of a Civic Guard

Strong Tea

Is the Holy Ghost Really a Kerryman?
   and Other Topics of Interest

The Gentle Art of Matchmaking
   and Other Important Things

Death Be Not Proud

JOHN B. KEANE

Letters
of a
Country Postman

THE MERCIER PRESS
DUBLIN & CORK

The Mercier Press Limited,
4 Bridge Street Cork,
25 Lower Abbey Street, Dublin 1.

ISBN 0 85342 496 9

To Monika and John Spillane

THE POSTMAN WRITES
TO HIS FRIEND HAMISH MacSHAMUS

The Ivy Cottage,
Lisnacoo,
Ballyfee.

Dear Hamish,

Steam is your powerful weapon. You can use it to heat homes and hospitals. With steam you can manufacture all kinds of metal. Bless my soul but you can drive a train with it or cook your supper with it and that's not all for if you have a sufficiency of curiosity and cunning you can read the minds of your neighbours with steam. You can discover their innermost thoughts and secret yearnings and the progress of their offspring and kinsfolk in distant places. You could write the history of a parish with steam and I ought to know for my immediate superior, my postmistress Katie Kersey, once mastered the use of steam, as no other before or since, for furthering her knowledge of the fortunes and misfortuntunes of those who dwelt within the bounds of her postal district.

The only instrument she used was a small aluminium kettle with a spout as slender and shapely as the youngest wand of a willow. From this spout, as the water in the kettle began to boil, there emanated a powerful jet of whistling steam strong enough to rise a blister on the most calloused palm or subtle enough to sever the flap from the most hermetically sealed envelope.

You may say here with justification that anybody with a kettle to hand could steam open an envelope. Agreed. However, it is not the manner of opening that matters for please to remember my dear Hamish that the letter must be closed again and in such a fashion that its ultimate recipient will have no idea that it has been tampered with.

Katie Kersey worked in absolute privacy. First she locked the door of her kitchen and from the depths of her apron extracted a small pincers. Then she rummaged through the mailbag until she located the letter she wanted. Using the pincers she took a tender hold and placed the prized epistle in the path of the escaping steam. Once while thus engaged she was seen through the kitchen window by an old woman who wished to make a phone call. Katie had neglected to draw the curtains. Later when she admitted the old woman she explained her actions:

'Toasting a taste of bread I does be there by the fire,' she said. As soon as the steam had softened the gum the flap curled outward and upward so that the letter within could be extracted without difficulty. For this purpose Katie used the pincers. What followed then amounted to a ritual. With infinite care as if they were breakable objects Katie would place the letter and the envelope near each other on the spotless surface of the kitchen table.

In the dresser the showpiece of a motley kitchenware collection was an ornate casserole adjudged by local experts to be a hundred years old and now far too fragile and cracked to suit the purpose for which it was originally intended. Lifting the cover Katie would gently withdraw a pair of immaculate white gloves, a Christmas present from a niece who is a member of a religious order. Delicately Katie would pull on the gloves smoothing them over her podgy hands like a surgeon readying himself for an important operation. Next came her spectacles, wire-rimmed with powerful lenses. These she polished with a fragment of convenient chamois. Time after time she puffed her moist breath upon the lenses, polishing them immediately after each puff until at last the requisite glossiness had been achieved. Then with a mighty sigh of contentment she would plop into her favourite chair to savour the contents of the letter. Sometimes she would content herself with one epistle. On other occasions she had an insatiable appetite and would read several at one sitting. Her knowledge of the postal district was all-embracing yet she never once revealed either by word or deed that she knew anything more than the simplest inhabitant of the place.

While Katie read she sobbed and sighed, moaned in distress, laughed in exulatation, frowned, smiled and scowled as she digested titbit after titbit, woe after woe, triumph after triumph, disaster after disaster. The moment a letter was finished it was re-sealed with the aid of the kettle and if necessary a smear or two of judiciously applied gum. These acts alone, however, were not enough. There were many in Lisnacoo who were not above examining letters under magnifying glasses to see if they had been tampered with. When the letter was closed Katie would place it at the corner of the table. Then with the aid of a chair she would sit on it with one of her ample buttocks. The whole fourteen stone of her was tilted on to this solitary buttock. It was a precarious balance but when the buttock was removed the letter was flat as a pancake and impregnably sealed to boot. Even the closest inspection failed to reveal any sign of interference.

Many is the sly smile that appeared on Katie's face and she sitting in the church on Sunday mornings. The saintlier and more sanctimonious the cummunicants the more knowing the smile. Often half aloud she would say to herself in a true spirit of justification as certain pious people returned with bent heads from the altar: 'Only God and myself knows the kind they really are.' Fair dues to her she kept her mind to herself except alone when her niece the nun arrived for a few days' holiday. Then all was revealed as the saying goes and as to whether it went any farther your guess is as good as mine although in all fairness regarding nuns there are those who fervently believe that the only word you'll get from one is the word of God. For the present all the best. See you in the summer D.V. Fond regards to the missus and family.

As ever,
Your oul' segocia,
Mocky Fondoo.

7

Sarsfield's Mews,
Upper Shoe Street,
Cork.

Dear Mocky,

I hope you remember me. I am the curly-haired young
fellow who used to follow you on your rounds through the
village of Liscnacoo and the postal district of Ballyfee. You
were always very kind to me when my parents and I were
on holidays down there. You remember I always told you I
would one day become a postman. At last that day has
dawned and after many an up and down I am off on my
first round next Monday morning. It's a country district
about three miles from the city. Of course I have a van
which is more than you ever had. What I would really
appreciate are a few basic tips about the snags which are
likely to beset me. I am most anxious to be a success at my
job the way you always were. You must be forty years at
the game now so anything you might have to convey to me
would be of help. Every good wish to you and yours.

Sincerely,
Frank O'Looney.

Wangle Avenue,
Off Sidberry Row,
Glasgow.

Dear Mocky,

This is to tell you I shan't be spending the holidays in Lisnacoo this summer. The wife wants to go to Malta. I'll miss
the fishing and the bit of poaching. What I'll miss most is
your company over the beer in the 'Lisnacoo Elms'. Not to
worry. We'll be back next year. You know it often occurred
to me to ask you about the women in your life. Uniforms,
they say, attract all types and I'm sure a postman's is no
exception. Write and tell me all the news when you get a
chance.

Your sincere friend,
Hamish MacShamus.

Sradbally Lower,
Ballyfee.

Dear Mocky Fondoo,

How is it I gets no letter at all and them lightin hures of Caffertys down the road gets several in the week and a big bundle at Christmas. Even the Feens that had all belong to them in an out of jail for robbery and buggery gets their share including parcels. What in God's name are you doing with my letters? I'll swear there is thousands of dollars gone astray or robbed from aunts of mine in America. One Christmas card I got entirely and that was a nice one from Cronin the butcher in Lisnacoo threatening me with law over three rack chops I swear I paid the thief for. Bring on my letters at once do you hear and the money that's inside in them or you'll hear about it.

Nance Nolan.

P. S. I see Katie Kersey at the chapel and she having a new coat. Your own wife is never short of style neither.

Nance Nolan.

The Ivy Cottage,
Lisnacoo,
Ballyfee.

Dear Hamish,

I agree that uniforms have a fatal fascination for certain women but a postman's more so than any you care to name. I'll grant you ours is a secure, pensionable position, respected by the public as few others are but there's a lot more to it than that. From the ages of fifteen to seventy in my range of experience I have seen sane, sensible women lose their heads over this humble uniform of mine. It's a sort of disease that blinds them to everyone else and they spend their time, after the germ invades, waylaying and inveigling innocent and no-so-innocent postmen. From the

9

day I delivered my first epistle I found myself in deep water with the opposite sex. When I wore civvies women tended to ignore me but when I went out into the world a fully-fledged, fully-uniformed postman I found myself in a new and deadly game. Of course, I was single then and not a bad-looking chap even if I do say so myself. I thought I knew it all but alas I was no match for some of the conniving dames along my route. The first odd bird I encountered was a buxom, black-eyed bundle of mischief in her thirties. She had three children who bore no resemblance whatsoever to each other which is no great surprise seeing as how she wasn't married. One morning I made the fatal mistake of offering her a cigarette. She accepted it as if it were a proposal of marriage. I had a terrible job keeping her at bay after that.

There was another, a sonsy widow, fair, fat and forty who would complain of having a severe pain in her belly every time I called to deliver her social insurance. First she asked me if I knew of any cure for it but after a while when we got to know each other better she wanted me to feel it to see if there were any dangerous lumps on it.

The worst I met was a fiery, red-haired Dexter at the southernmost end of Ballyfee postal district. She was the only daughter of departed parents and facing up to her fiftieth year like 'twould be her twentieth with a gait on her like a water-hen and a screech to match. In my first week she took a daft and unyielding fancy to me until I took to thrusting her letters under the door rather than confront her.

What did she do one day but send herself a registered letter which it was my solemn duty to deliver. I remember it was a fine day in June with a lovely blue sky that boded well for hay, the kind of day that a postman on his bicycle loves best of all. Against my will I dismounted as soon as I reached the entrance to her house. I knocked at the door but there was no response. I knocked a second time, louder and longer than the first but still there was no reply of any kind, not even the bark of a dog or the miaow of a cat. I

10

lifted the latch and peered into the kitchen but there was no sign of life. There was a fire in the Stanley and on it the kettle sang gently but no trace whatsoever of the damsel herself. I called out her name which was Gracie, Gracie Goddy she was nicknamed although her true title was Grace Godleigh. There was no answer. I opened the back door which led out into the haggard. Again I called out her name and threw in a few prolonged halloos for good measure. I came back into the kitchen clutching the letter in my hand. That's one of the cardinal rules of the post. A registered letter must be signed for. At the time a cat's paw would have suited me fine but there wasn't even a cat. No witnesses, animal, human or otherwise.

It was then I noticed the bedroom door ajar. I was nonplussed. I had no choice but to knock. Knock I did but there was no answer. I stood back a respectable way and peered in. If it gave me all I could do to fend off Gracie Goddy in the wide spaces of her kitchen it was odds on I'd have no chance at all in her bedroom. There she was with a large comb in her hand and she propped up on the bed like a mermaid on a headland with her red hair thrown down over her shoulders, loose and shiny and her two breasts as bare as a brace of outsize goose-eggs.

I knocked once more at the bedroom door. To do any more would be in excess of my duty.

'Come in lovie,' said Gracie in a sort of a sing-song.

'I can't,' I said, ''tis against regulations.'

She muttered an unprintable word about regulations. It wasn't for my hearing of course.

'Rules was made to be broken,' she called out.

'I have my job to think of,' said I.

'Alright,' she said resignedly after a while, 'I'll come down so.'

Down she came. I turned away and looked out the window. There was a blackbird picking worms in the haggard so I concentrated on his antics. I don't know what I'd have done only for him.

'Sign there,' I said pointing my thumb backwards over my shoulder to the registration slip which I had placed on the table.

'But sure I have no pen,' she pouted.

I closed my eyes and placed my indelible pencil on the table. I waited then for a decent space and threw the letter over my shoulder. I had to turn, however, to collect the receipt. I had one glimpse of her as I snatched the slip. All I recall is a blur of white, a sizeable blur. I bolted through the front door forgetting my pencil. I remember too hearing a great sigh coming from somewhere in the depths of Gracie Goddy. She got married about two years after to a small, bald-headed man who drove a wagon for Duffy's Circus. It is interesting to note that he wore a green uniform and peaked cap. They went to Australia after she sold her place.

Even after I married there were several who refused to throw in the towel. There is no doubt but that the uniform was at the back of it all. Better looking men than I such as vets, inseminators, insurance agents, seed salesmen and warblefly inspectors seemed to enjoy immunity. You could be a film star and escape without notice but pull on a postman's uniform and you were a target for every sex starved damsel in the district. If I availed myself of half the chances I was offered I'd be growing daisies for no man born of woman could possibly possess the energy to satisfy these famished females. Our local dispensary doctor is a man of the world by the name of Mongie. I asked him one night and we taking our pints in the 'Lisnacoo Elms' if he could explain this obsession with uniforms. He said it was probably a traditional thing, that over the years postmen seemed always to be set upon by dogs and women. I don't see how I can disagree with him. The man before me, Willie Liddy, was a notorious Lothario and the man before that was a bit of a playboy too. My immediate predecessor for all his conquests was crossed in love when he set about choosing a permanent partner. She was a farmer's daughter with her eyes set on land. She married land and left our man in the lurch. He went out of his mind for a while and suffered suspension as a result. He was found sitting one morning on Kilcoo Bridge with a powerful odour of whiskey all round him. His bag of letters was open on his lap. Every so often he would fling one on to the roadway and say: 'She loves me'. For every one he threw on the roadway he threw another into the river and cried: 'She loves me not'. In no time at all his bag was empty and he fell off to sleep by the bridge. Luckily the letters in the river floated long enough to be picked up by net fishermen in the estuary while the ones on the roadway were rescued by passers-by who quickly sobered up poor Willie and sent him off on his rounds. Ah dear I could go on all day about the uniform but alas I must now present myself to my postmistress, the one and only Katie Kersey or Katie the Steamer as the locals call her. From her I will collect the post, sort it with the only other postman in the district, my colleague Micky Monsell, then mount my bicycle and hit for the countryside of Ballyfee. Micky does the village of Lisnacoo and that part of Ballyfee which lies to the north of it while my territory consists of all the land to the south and west, a considerable area of approximately twenty square miles and roughly two hundred households.

I hope you enjoy the holiday in Malta. God knows we'll miss you this summer which incidentally will be my last one in the employ of the department of post and telegraphs. I'll be sixty-five in September and due to retire after fifty years in the service of the same employer.

For the time being I'll sign off. Regards to all.

As ever,
Your oul' segocia,
Mocky Fondoo.

Dear Frank,

Many thanks for yours of the fourteenth inst. Of course I remember you and I always knew you would be a postman one day. There are some men born to be postmen and I have no doubt but that you are one of those. It's hard to know where to begin if I am to advise you. There is no teacher like experience as you will find out but still a few pointers from an old stager might do no harm. You will find almost everything you need in the official rules and regulations but there's always more to a game than you'll find in the books. There are the things that cannot be written down. I will try to pinpoint trouble spots for you:

Number 1: Be discreet when you deliver a registered envelope. Let none look upon it except the person whose name it bears.

Number 2: When you deliver ordinary letters, if indeed any letter can be called ordinary, hand it to its legal owner face downwards if there are other persons present. This way neither the handwriting of the sender or the postmark can be seen.

Number 3: Never take tea in the same house two days in a row.

Number 4: Never let any particular house adopt you.

Number 5: Never appear drunk in uniform although at Christmas it's alright to be seen to be merry. People expect it of us.

Number 6: Always make sure you do not wear a uniform when becoming romantically involved with a woman.

Number 7: Keep one eye open for signs of want. There is much we can do.

Number 8: Remember well that there is no door so familiar that it can't do with a knock.

14

Number 9: Beware most of all of idle women. They'll play with you the way a cat plays with a mouse and often with consequences as dire.

Number 10: Never forget that in your sole custody are the innermost thoughts of the hundreds of souls entrusted to your care. In the most fragile and perishable of paper containers you transport tidings of priceless value for those to whom they are addressed. Remember that when a man entrusts his most private thoughts to paper he lays his reputation and character on the line. You sir carry his good name in your hands. This is the most valuable possession a man has. A man may reveal his sins in confession but he is capable of revealing all in his letters. In the last analysis he is dependant for discretion on you and you alone. Often you will convey expressions of the love that blossoms pure in the hearts of men and women. No trust could be more sacred. Transport these and all your other commissions with tenderness and care. I would forfeit my life rather than submit one of my letters to anyone but its rightful owner.

Number 11: Treat department inspectors as you would men from outer space, with caution, reserve and respect.

Number 12 and Last: Never forget that you are paid to deliver letters, not gossip.

I wish you luck and success in your career and I hope that what I have conveyed to you may be of some use of you. If you ever find yourself in a jam you'll know where to find me.

> As ever,
> Your oul' segocia,
> Mocky Fondoo.

Dear Mocky Fondoo,

I see you delivering at Feens yesterday. There was a bundle in your hand you hure and you goin' in. Who would be writin' to them Caffertys that had five out of their six daughters knocked up by travellers and soldiers and not a note of any sort for me as never did a thing out of the way to no one. There is fierce cuffuffling goin' on somewhere to say a woman of my standing does have to play second fiddle to disgenerates. All my letters are in a big heap somewhere hidden by villains in the post office or burned by those that begrudges me what is mine. The next person I'm goin' to see is the minister for post and telegraphs and we'll see how many will have jobs when I'm done.

Nance Nolan.

Dear Mocky,

I hate to bother you but I have no course left open to me other than writing to you. I know how persecuted you must be from people who think their letters are being mislaid and hold you to blame. I haven't heard from Jack in a fortnight which is unlike him. He was nearly always on the dot up till now and I can't understand why I haven't heard from him. It's not that I'm short of money. I have some spared out of what he sends me. Still it won't last much longer. Also I'm worried in case something has happened to him. I wrote to Miss Kersey the postmistress asking her if maybe the registered letter had gone astray. She answered by return and told me that there was no likelihood of such a thing and if there was that my husband would have the receipt and could make a claim.

Unfortunately this tells me nothing and so I am appeal-

ing to you. Would you enquire in the proper place for me
or look around in the sorting office to see if the letter was
mislaid. I'm worried sick Jack might have lost his job or
maybe he has had an accident. It's no fun with three young
children. Do what you can for me Mocky and I'll be forever
thankful to you.

Sincerely yours,
Kitty Norris.

The Ivy Cottage,
Lisnacoo,
Ballyfee.

Dear Hamish,
The fishing season opened yesterday and I landed a nice
nine pound cock fish with a two and a half inch blue and
silver in fairly high water. Others did not fare as luckily and
catches are well down on other years considering the
quality of the water. I am all alone at the moment. The
missus has gone to America to spend a holiday with my two
daughters who are married in New Jersey. She'll spend a
second period with my two sons in the Bronx. Altogether
she'll be gone three months. Although it's only a few days
since she boarded the plane at Shannon I already miss her
more than words can tell. All the crowd here send their
regards. You'll be missed in the taproom especially for the
chorus of *Loch Lomond*. The only news of importance is
that the postmistress's niece, Sister Gabrielle, is spending a
few days holiday with her beloved auntie. At night the pair
sit in the kitchen and Katie reveals all that there is to be
known about the fortunes of the people of the postal district of Ballyfee. To the casual listener it sounds as if a
litany is being recited with the nun offering short responses
every so often. What she is really doing is egging Katie on
when she hesitates before the jucier parts of her revelations.
She does not steam the letters open any more except on
very rare occasions. Very seldom indeed do I come across a

17

bum-flattened epistle these days. Every second house in the district has a telephone and all she has to do is listen. Sometimes, in an effort to catch her out, the party at the other end of the line might ask: 'Are you there Katie?'

Her answer to this is: 'You wouldn't be on the line you fool if I was elsewhere.' She misses nothing although she was nearly poisoned lately when she copied a cure for flatulence on to her pad. She keeps the pad handy when she is reciting for Sister Gabrielle. She looks to it for cues whenever she falters in the middle of a tale. The cure for flatulence consisted of a large dose of Cascara Sagrada mixed with boiled rhubarb. The whole thing was a set-up by a pharmicist's assistant working in Cork who happens to be doing an off-and-on line with a local flier. Otherwise she's a lovely girl in every way. It just so happens that some women are born cold, others warm and a rare few hot, a very necessary and sobering few for the survival of the sanity of that awful conglomerate known as the human race. Anyway our man was one night talking to the flier whose name I won't mention, not because I'm a gentleman or anything but beçause in my heyday I had a great appreciation for this type of young lady. While he was talking Katie was listening. Our man was at his most persuasive when our friend the flier expressed reluctance about spending a week-end in Cork. Our man reminded her of past joys and was becoming most elaborate in this respect when Katie cut him off without warning. She has her limits. Our friend was thus forced to make the long journey to Lisnacoo. His timing was wrong so he returned to Cork unappeased. While in Lisnacoo the flier informed him of Katie Kersey's doings and let it fall into the bargain that Katie was a chronic burper sounding off like a bull frog as I can personally verify from one end of the day to the other. During the course of the flier's next phone conversation with the pharmacist's assistant she asked him if he knew of a cure for flatulence intimating that her grandmother was a martyr to this noisy malady. The pharmacist's mate then

18

related the cure which he said was prescribed for Rose Kennedy by a Harley Street specialist.

Subsequently in the course of the morning between the hours of nine-thirty and twelve Katie Kersey paid a record number of nineteen visits to the toilet and did not quite make it on two.

They sit now at night herself and the saintly Sister Gabrielle while Katie recounts the broken engagements, the cross-channel abortions, the infidelities, the lusts and longings, the ups and downs of the Ballyfee subscribers and others further afield.

You may ask why people don't report her. The answer, of course, is that they might be saddled with worse and anyway what harm is she doing. There are meaner ways of getting one's kicks and but for the nun and I daresay a few of her cronies in the convent no one knows a damned thing. Another reason is that only part of what she hears is true and the young bucks of the parish have a habit of inventing unlikely tales for her titillation and their own amusement in the long winter nights. One day the parish-priest's housekeeper might be pregnant, a woman of sixty-three, another it might be the reverend mother of some convent. True or false Kittie would absorb all and relate all to the nun.

Katie is also probably the last of her kind. Her likes were as common as bogwater and I starting out but now for better or for worse they are gone from the scene. Reasons? Today people prefer to live their own lives. In Katie's hey-day in rural Ireland for the want of fulfilment and involvement they were forced to live other people's lives. It was that or go nuts. Only once ever did I see her lose her control. There's a fishing village about seven miles from here with a crowd of resident trawlermen who would do anything for diversion when the weather is unfit for fishing. One night they coaxed a Spanish colleague into making a phone call to Katie announcing that he was the new Papal Nuncio, Doctor Elbrigandi. Katie burped in surprise into the mouthpiece to be informed in broken English by Doctor Elbrigandi that she was being excommunicated for farting. Involuntarily she spluttered back with injured innocence that she was a burper not a farter but by this time the Spaniard had hung up on her. I'll close now as I have to tie a few minnows for Sunday's fishing. I have never lost so many. The river gets dirtier and snaggier every season and I often wonder how the salmon come up river at all. You'll be for Malta one of those days. Send a card if you think of it and while you're at it will you engage in an act of charity and send one to Miss Nance Nolan, Sradbally Lower, Ballyfee. Don't sign you own name. Just sign it 'The Knight of Malta'.

As ever,
Your oul' segocia,
Mocky Fondoo.

Sarsfield Mews,
Upper Shoe Street,
Cork.

Dear Mocky,
A thousand thanks for your letter and for the twelve good rules as Shakespeare said when referring to the game of Goose. Your advice should be pinned up in every post office in the country. What you wrote came to mind only last Thursday. I was delivering a seed catalogue to a farmer when his daughter chimed in and asked me to stay for a drop of tea. She asked me if I liked griddle bread and I said I adored it which is the honest to God truth. Every day since there is a cup of tea and a few slices of freshly made griddle bread waiting for me around lunchtime. Lately she has taken to adding a nicely boiled fresh egg. I can handle her, however. Make no mistake about it. By the way lest I forget. You said nothing about dogs in your list. Already I've received two bites and was lucky to escape without

several more. Every good wish to you and yours.

Sincerely,
Frank O'Looney.

Sradbally Lower,
Ballyfee.

Dear Mocky Fondoo,
Bad cess to yourself and Katie the Steamer for the robbin'
thieves that the pair of ye are. That's a great postboy is
Micky Monsell that does the other route. There's no fear he
passes a door. An I payin' Cronin the butcher yesterday for
rack chops and buyin' a bit of boilin' that decent postboy
lifted his cap and bade me the time of day. But I'm easy
now about yourself or Katie for who should write to me
only the Knight of Malta himself. You dassent interfere
with royal post like that. Maybe now you'll give the rest
and spare me the bother of writin' to the minister. No
wonder Katie does be smilin' and talkin' to herself and she
sittin' on her rump in the chapel with her leather coat and
who paid for your one's trip to America?

Nance Nolan.

The Ivy Cottage,
Lisnacoo,
Ballyfee.

Dear Kitty,
I am indeed sorry to report that there is no sign of a letter
from Jack, registered or otherwise in this post office. The
first light day's post I get in the coming week I'll call to
Sradbally but maybe you'll have news before that. I hope
the matter will be straightened out by then. If not I
shouldn't worry. The postal system is not foolproof and a
genuine mistake may have been made.

Your friend,
Mocky.

Dear Frank,

You're not a month on the job yet and already you have
broken one of my most important instructions. Don't ever
forget that I am fifty years at this caper. You say you
can handle this farmer's daughter who has the griddle bread
and boiled eggs waiting for you every day. That griddle
bread and those boiled eggs must be paid for and if you're
not careful my cocksure friend you'll find yourself picking
up the tab. What amuses me is your belief that you can
handle her. You will find to your cost if you're not careful
that it's a lot easier to handle nitro-glycerine. Can't you see
she's spinning a web made of eggs and griddle bread, a web
from which there is no escape once you tangle with its
weakest strand? I know the pattern like the back of my
hand. Next thing now you'll be getting trifle or roasted
apples or semolina pudding on top of the eggs and griddle
bread or maybe you have a preference for something special
like apple tart and cream or mandarin oranges. Have no
worries. She'll find out what it is and that will be another
strand around your throat. Can't you realise you're walking
a tightrope? Give yourself a chance, before you settle down,
to wear the arse off one pair of pants at least. Remember
what I said in my letter. Never take tea under the same roof
two days in a row. Yet here you are taking tea and more
besides in spite of all my warnings.

So you've been bitten by dogs. Will you tell me which
postman has not? Every one of us must adopt his own
strategy for dealing with this menace. No two dogs are alike
but every dog, behind the façade of viciousness, is a coward.
My predecessor, Willie Liddy, was badly bitten by a mongrel cow-dog on his first day out. Willie was anything but a
patient man. After the bite he ignored the dog and went
looking for its master. When he found him he left the im-

pression of a size eleven boot on the fellow's behind.

'If that dog bites me again,' Willie warned him, 'you're a dead man.'

The dog never bit him again. In this business it is wrong to blame the dog. The master or mistress must always be held to blame. My colleague Micky Monsel who delivers in the northern half of the district is nicknamed Dogmeat for the simple reason that dogs will not leave him alone. Wandering curs recognise him when he's off duty and single him out for attack. In uniform he has no peace at all. For some years now he wears wellingtons to protect his calves and ankles from the fangs of his tormentors. Certain postmen are unfortunate in this respect. Some aspect of their appearance, attitude or manner seems to bring out the worst in otherwise well-behaved dogs. Even suave, elderly, well-bred dogs with pedigrees are transformed into snarling savages the moment Dogmeat Monsell lifts the latch on the gate where they stand with innocent faces looking as if the last thought in their heads was the biting of a postman. Approval and welcome are written all over them. They are the types of dog one instinctively pats on the head, dogs with honest, good-natured faces, faces that inspire trust and confidence. Yet the moment Dogmeat turns his back a terrible transformation takes place. Dogmeat has a theory that people use postmen as guinea-pigs in order to turn harmless mutts into watchdogs.

With me it's different. I like dogs and get on fairly well with all types. Occasionally I meet an exception but I have a pre-arranged strategy for dealing with these. I look them in the eye and keep looking them in the eye until they skulk off with hangdog looks. There are rare occasions when this does not work and when one meets a really nasty mongrel the owner must be confronted and told that until such time as the dog behaves deliveries must be suspended. With some dogs I have struck up lasting friendships and these follow me on my route until the domain of another dog is reached. Here I am handed over to the dog in charge who in turn will escort me to the bailiwick of the next dog. Often I have been attacked for no reason by pairs of dogs and on occasion by packs of three or four. The exercise here is to isolate the ringleader and concentrate all your energies on him.

However, no matter what precautions a postman may take there is no guarantee of immunity. Alas all the suspicion and mistrust is on one side. It is in the nature of a dog to express hostility towards callers but especially towards postmen so it has to be the uniform. 'But,' you may say, 'has not a Civic Guard a uniform?'

He has but he also has a baton and whatever a dog may do it is not likely he will attack a man who has a weapon. More important, owners see to it that their dogs are on their best behaviour whenever a Civic Guard calls around so we may conclude that the owner is every bit as cunning as the dog. I am firmly of the belief that there should be some sort of compatibility or competence test before a person is allowed to take charge of a dog because I have often found that there is more animal in the man than there is in the dog. Often too a sensitive dog can read his master's face and upon seeing worry or fear inscribed thereon, because of the impending visit of a postman, may foolishly presume that the postman is an enemy. Those who receive letters every day take letters for granted but a man who never receives a letter has good reason to fear one when it is delivered unexpectedly. Of course there is a chance in a million that he may have inherited money. More likely, however, it is a bill or some other request for money from friends or relations. Just as in newspapers and other forms of the communications media there is more bad news than good news in letters. Therefore, to the one-letter-a-year-man the postman has to be the bearer of bad tidings. He may avoid the Civic Guard or the process server by the simple expedient of skipping out the back door and spending his day in the wilds until danger has passed. He cannot do this with the postman because there is always the outside chance that the letter may contain good tidings or because of the million to one chance that it may contain news of a legacy. While hope keeps springing in the human breast there is always the possibility that news of a legacy may spring from the postman's bag. That's all for now except to issue a final warning. Better men than you were collared by tea and griddle bread.

> As ever,
> You oul' segocia,
> Mocky Fondoo.

P. S. It wasn't Shakespeare who referred to the twelve good rules and the royal game of Goose. It was Oliver Goldsmith, the same man who referred to every fool in the countryside from swain to parson but made sure to say nothing about the postman. We have accounts of cripples, schoolmasters, spendthrifts, geese and watchdogs but no mention of you know who.

> M. F.

> Templebawn,
> Ballyfee.

Dear Mister Fondoo,
I hesitates ere I writes to you as my matter is most private. I was expecting a small parcel with special goods in it which has not come. As it was medicine would you treat it with care and not open it don't all the good go out of it.

> Yours sincere friend,
> Catríona Cooney (Mrs).

> Sradbally Upper,
> Ballyfee.

Dear Mocky,
I cannot thank you enough for calling and for your kind offer. I have written to my mother for help. She's fairly

well off. I'm certain that Jack is in hospital somewhere suffering from loss of memory. I have written to the Roman Catholic Parish Priest of his district and to a few other people I know. It's a bit too soon to notify the police. There were other times when a few weeks went by without hearing from him and once a month passed without my getting a copper. It was the time he hurt his leg. The letter you brought the last day was unsigned. It was from someone in the neighbourhood who seems to know an awful lot about me and about Jack. It was a dirty letter. Thanks again for all your help. I hope we hear from Jack soon as I'm getting really worried.

Yours sincerely,
Kitty Norris.

The Ivy Cottage,
Lisnacoo,
Ballyfee.

Dear Hamish,
I don't know where to begin. The news has been piling up. The latest is that the last of the Burley sisters has married into another big farm west of Lisnacoo to a bachelor gay by the name of Jack Silky who is up to the top of his two hairy ears in debt. The Burley lady had the money, however, and the mystery here is where she came by it and indeed where did her sisters come by it for the four of them are married into the biggest farms in these parts. Many is the registered letter I delivered to their mother across the years but what could be inside I asked myself except a few pounds at most. The Burleys you see were illiterate and spent most of their growing years avoiding the classroom. Where then did they make the thousands when all that any of them spent in London was two years? For me the mystery was solved the other night in the 'Lisnacoo Elms' when the last of the Burleys stood me a drink the night before the wedding, slipped me a fiver too and thanked me

for the faithful way I had delivered her earnings to the mother. She was half drunk and as the night wore on she grew drunker still.

'You did well in England,' I said cautiously.

'Better than I'd ever do here,' she said.

'Were you in service?' I asked.

'You might say I was,' she replied with a smirk.

I smirked as well but I kept my mouth shut.

'The Burleys mightn't be able to work the brain so good,' said she proud as you please, 'but they makes up for it by working the other thing.'

I got the message but I feigned ignorance. She sighed at my innocence.

'What I often gave away here,' said she, 'for a fist of gooseberries or a fag I gets a score of notes for over there.'

On the tragic side there's a lovely woman living in Sradbally Upper. Her name is Kitty Norris and it would seem that her husband has deserted her. I think the truth may be dawning on her at last. She has also been receiving anonymous letters from a gentleman in the area. I think I may know who he is. He fakes the writing but it isn't easy pull the wool over the eyes of a postman. Jack Norris was always a bit of a playboy. He gave up a good job here to go to England where he said the pickings were better. How any man could leave a woman like Kitty Norris is beyond me. I fear he has taken up residence with another woman which, alas, is not an uncommon practice with those who leave their wives behind when they go abroad. The trouble is that there was no need for Jack to go. He seems now to have deserted poor Kitty and from here on she will be dependant on her mother for the bite and sup or any other charity which might come her way. What a fall this is for a proud and lovely girl. I remember when she first came to Sradbally Upper as a young bride. She brightened the kitchen with her blushes and the countryside with the sound of her voice. What madness possesses grown men to forsake such beauty?

Last week I was reported to the postmistress by a Mrs Catríona Cooney of Templebawn. The postmistress has no real authority over me if I wanted to go by the book. The head postmaster is my real boss. Katie, in turn, reported me to the postmaster. What happened was this. A small box addressed to Mrs Cooney was damaged in transit and had to be returned to the district office for re-parcelling. The district postmaster is a man by the name of Mallvey. He is an ex-army man, fond of strong drink and strong language but as genuine a scout as you could meet. Many's the postman he saved from suspension. When I entered his office he was looking out the window, standing with his hands on his hips. There was an overseer by the name of Dick Cavill seated at a table on which was a small cardboard parcel which had almost disintegrated because of bad parcelling and rough handling.

'What do you make of that Mocky?' Mallvey said without turning his head.

'Don't know sir,' I told him.

'Pick up the shagging thing,' he said, 'and examine it. Tell me what you see.'

I lifted the parcel. I groped inside and withdrew some of the contents.

'Now what do you make of it?' Mallvey said turning around.

'French letters,' I said.

'Exactly,' said Mallvey. 'Bloody well disgraceful using the Post for such purposes. Now Mocky I must ask you a question. Did you open this parcel?'

'No sir. I've never seen it before now. Katie never showed it to me.'

'That's good enough for me,' said Mallvey. 'Do your duty Dick,' he addressed the overseer.

'Very good sir,' said Cavill. 'What method shall I use to dispose of them sir?'

'Consign them to flames,' the postmaster's voice was full of mock indignation, 'and see that every last one is burned

28

to a frazzle.'

'Yes sir,' said Dick obediently.

'They'll be mounting them bareback in Templebawn till the next consignment comes,' the postmaster quipped.

I followed Dick Cavill downstairs to the basement where there was a furnace. On his way he transferred the contents of the package to his own person.

'Witness this,' he said to me as he flung the empty package into the flames. 'Witness the destruction of these instruments of depravity, these sheaths of iniquity. The lechers of Templebawn will be without sport tonight. I swear to that on the eighty-two balls of Ali Baba and the Forty Thieves. Come on, we'll have a drink somwhere before I drive you home.'

I remember well the time when we had a list of banned newspapers and magazines pinned up in all offices. There was the *News of the World, Truelife Detective, The Naked Truth* and several others. The clerks in the district office and their wives and relations had great reading in those days, those of them that were interested in pictures of naked men and women and true tales of bigamy, rape, murder, sadism, bestiality, buggery, infidelity and other uncommon doings too numerous to mention.

The publications I mention would nearly always be con-cealed inside religious magazines or British newspapers which were deemed acceptable by the censors. When they were well wrapped and hidden so that no sign of them was revealed they would find their way to the people to whom they were addressed. When they were not it was the duty of the postal clerks and sorters who handled them to take them from their wrappings and destroy them. The sorters and clerks were not fools so they took the magazines home or gave them to friends who were in dire need of diversion in the long nights of winter. Sometimes they burned them but only when they were read by all who had wanted to read them. The Irish censors must have been the most naïve and backward men of any age in the Island of Saints and

29

Scholars. It was a poor post office that hadn't a comprehensive library of banned magazines in those benighted days. I'll sign off now. I must write to the wife and fill her in on all the goings-on of Lisnacoo and greater Ballyfee no matter how trivial. She doesn't write at all herself. She's a bad speller and her hand is illegible. She had a mild stroke some years ago as you know. For the present then Hamish all the very best.

As ever,
Your oul' segocia,
Mocky Fondoo.

Sarsfield Mews,
Upper Shoe Street,
Cork.

Dear Mocky,

You were right about the drawing power of the uniform. I'm fighting them off as best I can. No need to worry about the damsel who provides the boiled eggs and the griddle bread. Her name is Rosanna McDoogle. One of the clerks in the head office here was marking my card the other night but he made no mention of Rosanna so she's no tracker. Only last Thursday she had my favourite feed waiting for me when I struck the house at dinnertime. I could eat spare ribs and cabbage from morning till night. I must have let it drop, in passing, that I liked them for the plate was piled high with ribs of the finest quality. There is no danger of my getting involved in a serious way. This is a decent sort who just wants to be friends.

Friday last she asked me to bring out a parcel of bikinis on appro from the city. I won't have a chance till Saturday afternoon. She has promised she'll let me select the most suitable one on Monday when I call. She plans to go abroad for a fortnight in July. We have a great chat when I call. There never seems to be anybody around although she has brothers and sisters and both parents living. She is the oldest of the family. She says she's only twenty-eight but I suspect she's a bit older.

I'll remember what you wrote about cross dogs. The man who retired from this route just before I was appointed always carried a small ash plant. He struck first and asked questions afterwards. Dogs left him alone. I don't want to go around trailing an ash plant so I'll try your methods.

Have no worries about my marrying Rosanna McDoogle or anybody else for ten years at least. I'll wear the arse off twenty pairs of pants before I join the ranks of the martyrs.

Sincerely,
Frank O'Looney.

P. S. Was there a postman by the name of Bugler McNulty. I mean did he really exist and was he the character people make him out to be?

Frank.

Sradbally Lower,
Ballyfee.

Dear Mocky Fondoo,
No letter. No parcel. No card. I wrote to the Knight of Malta and I got no answer. I wrote to know would he have any old suits for my brother Dan or shoes and know would his wife have any summer dresses that she had no use for but divil the word. The Knight's clothes would suit Dan. Our Dan is the dead stamp of Prince Philip. Don't do away with this parcel like you did the others.

Nance Nolan.

Wangle Avenue,
Off Sidberry Row,
Glasgow.

Dear Mocky,
Just back from Malta, nice and brown. So is the wife. In

31

no way can it be compared with Lisnacoo and Ballyfee with the mountains all around and the green, green fields and the waterfalls not to mention the people. Now that the wife's whim is fulfilled it's Lisnacoo for me for evermore. I sent your friend a Maltese calendar and a sheaf of brochures. Should keep her quiet for a while. Sorry to hear about that nice woman in Sradbally Upper. I remember her. Old lechers like myself don't easily forget a face and a figure like that. You'll find a gift under separate cover. It's only a wooden cross but it's artistic and it's peculiar to the island where it was made. Tonight I intend to write to the 'Lisnacoo Elms' booking my spot for next year. I'm tired so I'll close for the moment. I look forward to hearing from you.

Your sincere friend,
Hamish MacShamus.

The Ivy Cottage,
Lisnacoo,
Ballyfee.

Dear Frank,

I grow more amused at your assessment of Rosanna McDoogle. Will you take my word for it that an eligible bachelor can be anything with an eligible spinster except good friends. Such a relationship between a man and a woman may last for a short while but, because of the nature of the bashte, as the saying goes, must exceed the bounds of friendship in a matter of time. Keep that in mind when you're measuring Rosanna for bikinis. Believe me Frank if you had no job and no uniform you'd be as much in demand by the Rosanna McDoogle's of this country as a Christmas tree in the middle of January. Try to stand back and have an objective look at your exact position. You're lunching at McDoogle's regularly at considerable expense to oul' McDoogle you may be sure. You are selecting bathing costumes for Rosanna. Does it not strike you as sinister or odd to say the least that there is no member of

32

the McDoogle family present while you are on the premises
stuffing your gut with spare ribs and cabbage? Does it not
strike you as odd that they receive a letter or letters every
day of the week? What important role in the community
does oul' McDoogle play to say that he's barricaded with
letters every day of his life? In normal circumstances a
small farmer like McDoogle might receive a letter once a
week. I can see McDoogle clearly in my mind's eye. There
he is, saddled with a wife and large family with the eldest
daughter Rosanna showing every sign of becoming a permanent fixture. This is a state of affairs which can be
intolerable in a small house where it is no fun making ends
meet. Oul' McDoogle is driven almost to the point of dis-
traction. The wife turns to novenas. Suddenly the prayers
are answered and salvation in the shape of a rookie postman
appears out of the blue. Spick and span with his yellow van
and his new uniform he is too precious a catch to be sought
after with ordinary bait. Here's a man with a fine pensionable position, a civil servant and a respected figure to crown
all. We want a big net with small meshes for this fish. However it's not yet too late. Pull out now before your paunch
is pulled to the ground by spare ribs. Don't hesitate for
another moment. You are in grave danger. At least give
yourself a chance to put your first Christmas on the job
behind you as a single man. You're too young for marriage.
Great God you're not yet twenty-one years of age and
already you're on the point of being hooked for life.

You ask about the Bugler McNulty. Yes he existed,
Patrick Augustine Stanislaus McNulty, pride of the auxili-
aries and the terror of overseers, with more suspensions to
his credit than any ten postmen anywhere. You could, I
suppose, call him a lover of the outdoors if only for the
good reason that he slept more often out of doors than
indoors, rarely ever being sober enough to find his own way
home. He mislaid, lost and damaged hundreds of parcels
and letters. Yet he was never sacked, the chief reason being
that he was rarely reported by his victims. He was un-

believably popular. Despite having a mountainous and circuitous route he started his first day without a bicycle. On his first assignment he headed straight for the local creamery where outlying farmers came with their milk every morning. Here he would distribute most of the letters to their proper owners and to neighbours of the owners who would deliver them, if they remembered, as they returned home from the creamery. Most of the letters were delivered one way or another in due course but, unfortunately, a small number fell into the wrong hands and here is where the Bugler's troubles started. Here is what happened.

Not all the farmers would go directly home from the creamery. A few would spend most of the day in the nearest public house playing rings or darts or maybe debating the progress of national and international affairs. Outside horses, ponies and asses were tethered to telephone poles, church railings or to each other. Some owners thoughtfully provided their animals with bundles of hay but most of the unfortunate creatures just stood there resignedly and patiently until their masters could drink no more or until their monies were exhausted.

All this time important letters for neighbours lay forgotten in their pockets. Upon reaching home, well and truly befuddled by drink, a member of the household would see to the untackling of the horse or pony while the lord and master sat down to his dinner. After dinner he would generally be overcome by drowsiness so he would either park himself by the fire or take a turn in the bed. Not all wives would rummage through his pockets while he slept but there were a few who would, a few who hungered for news and companionship, who lived in semi-isolation, in desolation and despair, whose loveless marriages were poor fodder for the hunger and loneliness. For these there was nothing to whack the reading of a neighbour's letter to lift one out of the blues. It was easily located and read. Lacking the subtle craftmanship of Katie Kersey the women in question were left with no option but to destroy the letters once they were read.

Inevitably complaints came in and an investigation followed. The upshot of the ruction was that the Bugler was suspended for a fortnight and cautioned that if he ever again broke the rules he would be dismissed. He promised the postmaster that he would never visit the creamery again. He was true to his word. From that time forward he let it be known that those who wanted letters for themselves, their friends or their neighbours might obtain same by visiting a certain public house where he would be in residence from morning till night. Not only did this arrangement simplify the Bugler's task but it also resulted in his being stood round after round of free drinks from grateful clients, particularly those in receipt of registered letters or those who did not want their spouses to know that they were receiving letters.

It could not last and following complaints the Bugler was called before his postmaster. He was asked to defend his actions.

'You told me to stay away from the creamery and I did,' the Bugler said.

'But I didn't tell you go to the pub,' the postmaster pointed out.

'You didn't,' the Bugler replied, 'but you didn't tell me stay away from it either.'

'Damn you,' the postmaster shouted. 'You know the rules. You took an oath.'

'I know. I know,' the Bugler said placatingly, 'but I'm not able for the long journey into the hills.'

'You have a bicycle,' the postmaster reminded him.

'It's punctured,' the Bugler told him.

'You have an allowance of one and sixpence a week to maintain that bicycle,' the postmaster persisted.

'You wouldn't maintain a pair o' drawers on one and six a week,' the Bugler replied.

'Every other postman with a rural route uses his bike without complaint so why shouldn't you?'

'It makes me dizzy when I mount up,' the Bugler responded.

'Then you'd better be on the lookout for a job that won't make you dizzy,' the postmaster said. The Bugler made no reply to this. He sat there, wordless, with his head in his hands. From time to time he would look beseechingly at the postmaster who was a soft-hearted man behind the façade of authority. A large tear left the Bugler's eye and proceeded slowly down his face towards the side of his mouth where he demolished it with his tongue. He looked for all the world like an old hound slobbering for mercy before its master. The postmaster turned his head away. The Bugler was re-instated after a fortnight and for a while his work was exemplary. Then one day he mislaid his bag. When he reported for work the following morning he could give no account of it. He was suspended for a month at the end of which time he recovered the bag from under a bed in the house of a widow where he often spent more time than was necessary. Not a letter had she touched. All were eventually delivered and as the Bugler put it when he was once again confronted by his postmaster: 'A late letter is better than no letter at all.' For the present I'll bid you adieu and hope you come to your senses soon in respect of Miss Rosanna McDoogle.

As ever,
Your oul' segocia,
Mocky Fondoo.

Sradbally Upper,
Ballyfee.

Dear Mocky,

Sorry to trouble you with my burdens. I will hand this letter to the first passer-by in the hope that it reaches you before you set out on your rounds tomorrow morning. I hate asking you but I have nobody else to ask. My mother is in hospital after an operation and won't be out and about

36

for another week at least. Would you bring the following items with you if you can fit them on the carrier; a half pound of tea, a quarter stone of sugar, a half stone of flour or three large pan loaves, two boxes of matches, a half pound of margarine and a pound or so of lean bacon. I never thought I would see the day that I'd have to beg from a friend.

I'll pay you back in a week or so when I hear from my mother.

Yours sincerely,
Kitty Norris.

The Ivy Cottage,
Lisnacoo,
Ballyfee.

Dear Hamish,
Steam, we are told, is the first man-made source of power and is there anything, I ask you, as incomparably efficient as the steam turbine. The first tiny turbine was invented about nineteen hundred years ago by Hero of Alexandria but I strongly suspect that steam was used as a source of power before that. We are told that as far back as two and a half thousand years before Christ the Egyptians were making good quality paper from a reed called Papyrus. Now, if they were making paper you may be sure they were writing letters and if they were writing letters they were using envelopes or, if not, some glutinous or sticky substance was being used to seal their private communications and secret dispatches. If this was the case, and there is no historical evidence to suggest otherwise, we can take it for granted, human nature being what it is, that steam was in wide use in Egypt and thereabouts so that curious people might acquaint themselves with the correspondence of their friends, neighbours and relations.

You may wonder why I open on this note. The reason my dear Hamish is that there is a return to steam as a source of power in the kitchen of Katie Kersey, the postmistress of Lisnacoo. The evidence is overwhelming. We are in the middle of a telephone strike so that all news from that source has dried up. Also when the laundry van called here a few evenings back I noticed among Katie's aprons and bibs one pair of gloves, immaculately white. The kitchen door is locked for long periods and the curtains are drawn. Finally, to set the seal in favour of my suspicions, a number of letters addressed to prominent people are bottom-flattened to such a degree that you could say with absolute certainty they were autographed by the large left buttock of Katie Kersey. Like Michelangelo or Picasso her work is unmistakable.

The trouble is that while Katie's style is instantly recognisable the standard has dropped far below those fine classical examples of her pre-telephone period. Her finished work has now become sloppy and careless. One still encounters the occasional epistle where the master buttock of the craftsman can be seen but these are isolated cases and, by and large, those letters which are not partly open are often only partly closed. Age has caught up with her and unless her work improves or the strike ends quickly more than her age will be catching up with her. I don't want to see this happen so I may take steps myself if the worst comes to the worst. I happen to know that the nun is due next week-end and it could be that in her anxiety to tank up with a full complement of news Katie is rushing her work with the result that there is carelessness. At the moment there is a run of watery gum on the market or so I tell those who look with jaundiced eyes on their letters. They all know Katie's form and many have devised simple code systems to safeguard important communications. Cracking codes is child's play to a woman with Katie's cunning and experience. The harder the code the more fun she knocks out of it.

Six more weeks and I'll be a free man. It's about time after fifty years. Still my friends on the route tell me, out of the goodness of their hearts no doubt, that I don't look a day over fifty. It's nice to hear it even if there's no truth in it. I understand the lads in the district office and my colleagues are to make me a presentation followed by a booze-up and buffet at the 'Lisnacoo Elms'. Dogmeat Monsell is in charge of the affair and every man, woman and child in his route know all about it. That's all for now my dear Hamish. Best regards to the wife. Write soon.

Your oul' segocia,
Mocky Fondoo.

Sarsfield Mews,
Upper Shoe Street,
Cork.

Dear Mocky,

Still single and will be for many a long year to come. You're a born pessimist that's what you are. We picked out a lovely red bikini. You could fit the lot into a small envelope. It was a tricky job but we managed in the finish. We tried several before finding the right one. What a figure this girl has. Maybe she's a bit big around the hips but what of it. I've never come across the likes of her in all my born days. 'Tis a case of no holds barred in dead earnest. Rosanna McDoogle is the fastest piece of goods since the first ray of light penetrated the darkness of the universe. I have it all and it's costing nothing, spare ribs, griddle bread, the works. You were right Mocky. You said she'd come up with what I like best of all and she has. Thanks for all your help and advice.

Sincerely,
Frank O'Looney.

P. S. Why was the Bugler McNulty so called? You made no reference to a bugle in your letter.

Frank.

Dear Brigid,

The house isn't the same without you. Indeed life isn't the same without you. I long for the hour when you'll be back in our bed again. 'Tis a black spot, is this place since you went. The only other creature, apart from myself, who comes and goes is the cat. Other than him there is nothing and at every hand's turn there is some little thing to keep reminding me of you. I heard from Hamish MacShamus. He's back from his holiday in Malta and seems to have enjoyed himself although Lisnacoo is still his favourite haunt and he hopes to be with us next year.

There isn't a whole heap of news. Fishing is poor and we constantly ask ourselves have we seen the last of the Atlantic salmon. The river is no place for such handsome and elegant visitors in these dirty times.

The stalks of the new spuds are showing well and should be in their prime against the time you come home. I sat a half hundred of cabbage and 'tis coming strong too.

'Tis only now that you're gone I realise the full truth of the old saying that a woman's work is never done because, God knows, there is always something to do around a house and when you think you have the last job done you find the next job facing you. The post is easy work by comparison.

I have the turf cut and futted and, please God, the pair of us will enjoy the heat and the sparkle of it across the winter. The hens are laying as good as ever, the cow milking well and the cat has a shine on him for I have him spoiled entirely.

It won't be long now and I'll be taking off this uniform forever. The post was a trade I loved from the first day I slung the mailbag across my shoulders but there comes a time to end a thing and to tell you the truth I find myself

40

yielding a little lately so 'twill be an ease when I retire. With the help of God we'll knock many a good day out of it yet.

On the black side of it poor Gracie Goddy's husband is dead but word has it she'll marry the second man at once if she can lay hold of him.

The last of the six Cafferty girls is knocked up. The blame is with a lorry driver, they say, who used deliver carrots and onions in Lisnacoo. Others hold the guilty man to be a wisp of a fellow who plays a tin whistle with a travelling folk group. He's that small you'd wash him in a saucepan but accounts have it he's the sire of a score or more since he took to the road. Appearances are the last thing a body should go by in the judgment of a man. Look at this ferret that would hardly bait a mouse-trap yet by all accounts he can put the come-hither on all and sundry and leave his mark besides.

Kitty Norris's husband seems to have deserted her. That's the talk anyway.

There is trouble looming for Katie Kersey unless the telephone strike ends quickly. She is opening letters at random now but worst of all she sometimes omits to return all the pages to the envelope. Later when she finds a lost page under the table or blown by a draught of wind to the top of the dresser she forgets where it came from. Other times she reads a rake of letters at a sitting but she returns them to the wrong envelopes so that Maggie Cafferty might be in receipt of Katie Feen's letter or vice versa. Susie Dill, the Flier, might receive our parish priest's, Father Kimmerley's letter or worst of all, God between us and all harm, poor Father Kimmerley might find himself reading a red hot love letter from that pharmacist's assistant below in Cork city. 'Tis a cruel mix-up. The complaints have started to pour into the district office. If Katie only paid more attention to the replacement of the letters and the re-sealing of the envelopes all would be well. People would have their suspicions but there is damn all you can do with a suspicion only be addling yourself from day to day and maybe grievously wronging innocent people.

There is little more I can think of offhand except to give my love to the children and to my grandchildren. There is no need for you to answer this or to bother with any sort of a letter or card until you're ready to come home. I'll have all things ready and will be at Shannon to greet you. Dogmeat Monsell will drive me down. That will be the happy day for me. For the present now take good care of yourself and if there is anything you want let me know and you won't be wanting it long.

> Love as always,
> Your devoted husband,
> Mocky.

> Guess Where,
> Ballyfee.

Poor Mocky,

While the cat's away the mice will dance. What did Kitty Norris give you in return for the messages you took her. It must be a great thrill for an old fellow of your age with hardly enough ribs to cover the small of his poll. They say women get a great kick out of baldy men. The best thrill of all they say is to rub the head of a baldy man. You can feel his brains underneath and tell what he might be thinking. Ha—ha! You should have more sense cocky Mocky at your age. Don't you know sex is bad for the hearts of the aged. What a pity if you should expire before you retire.

> Guess Who?

> Sradbally Lower,
> Ballyfee.

Dear Mocky Fondoo,

It must have broke your heart to hand in the parcel from the Knight of Malta last week. There was lovely books in it

42

that my brother Dan is reading those days but no sign of
the summer dresses or the suits I asked him for in my letter.
I hope they don't go astray like all the other parcels that
was sent to me or fall into wrong hands. If the cap fits
yourself and Katie can wear it.

Nance Nolan.

The Ivy Cottage,
Lisnacoo,
Ballyfee.

Dear Frank,

The Bugler McNulty as I told you was born Patrick Augustine Stanislaus McNulty. His parents died when he was a
gorsoon of ten. With the remainder of his brothers and
sisters he was sent to an orphanage. He escaped and worked
for a farmer until he was fourteen. Then he joined the army.
When he left the army he was appointed an auxiliary postman. He was christened the Bugler not long after his second
suspension. As was to be expected he behaved in a model
fashion for a short period after this suspension. In his ex-
tensive route there were several major crossroads created
for the most part by lesser, uncharted by-ways which
crossed a major road at intervals. These uncharted by-ways
might ramble into the hills for miles until they had serviced
the last of the houses in the hinterland.

The Bugler let it be known after a while to those con-
cerned that he had no notion of cycling or trudging to these
out of the way dwellings so he bought a policeman's whistle
in a second-hand shop in Cork. At each crossroads he would
blow this whistle to let the inhabitants of the far-off cots
know that the postman had arrived. But, you may ask, was
there not the likelihood that the whistle would bring the
inhabitants of every cot within whistle-range to the cross
roads rather than just those for whom the Bugler had letters?
Quite so. In the avoidance of his duties I must hand it to
the Bugler for the man was never less than brilliant. Let us

suppose that there were seven houses in that area of roadway or by-way stretching from the crossroads to the last
house and let us suppose that he had letters for the first,
third and sixth houses.

He would blow on the whistle, one long blast for number one house. Then he would pause for several seconds
before blowing three blasts for number three house. Then
would come another pause before letting go six blasts to
notify house number six.

Alas this system worked only on fine days when the
whistle blasts carried without difficulty to the ends of the
roadways. However should there be a breeze the end houses
could not pick up the sound. Should there be a gale not
even the first house could pick up the sound. There was no
option open then to the Bugler except to deposit all the
letters in house number one until such time as they were
called for by the inhabitants of numbers two to seven. This
was alright where the owner of number one house would
not steam open a letter or two to satisfy her curiosity.

Again it was a situation that could not last and the
Bugler was once more suspended. Still there was no doubt
that through trial and error his methods were becoming
more sophisticated. After the whistle he invested in a bugle.
He bought it off a man who used to play the last post over
the graves of members of the old I.R.A. This unfortunate
man had his jaw broken in a row over politics so the bugle
was of no more use to him. On his first day out after his
summer holidays the Bugler McNulty sounded his bugle at
the first crossroads. Two hares broke from the nearby
hedge and birds of all shapes and sizes burst from the
bushes at either side of the road. The sound of the bugle,
however, carried quite clearly to the end house despite the
fact that there was a fresh wind blowing down the path of
its notes. Only when a gale force wind blew was the sound
of the bugle inaudible. Gales were infrequent enough and at
last the Bugler McNulty was happy. His system was almost
foolproof. It lasted for several months or precisely until the

week before Christmas when the Bugler, who was well and truly sotted after liberal doses of whiskey, stout and poitcheen began to mix his notes. In addition there was no interval between them. The drinking lasted for a week and caused no end of trouble to the hill people. Inevitably there was a complaint and Dick Cavill was sent out from the district office. He found the Bugler in an advanced state of drunkenness under a holly bush and he endeavouring with all his might to blow his horn. Naturally he was suspended but the district office was always proud of him and at union meetings throughout the country clerks and others would boast of his exploits to anyone prepared to listen. He only used the Bugle in emergencies after that. So now you know why he was called the Bugler McNulty.

How is your girlfriend Rosanna? I have the distinct feeling that the time of the spare ribs and griddle cake is coming to an end. Don't ask me how. I know. I have a sixth sense about these things.

I have issued enough warnings so that the pitfalls should be quite clear to you. However I will say this. It is never too late to escape the clutches of any woman but to do this the sternest kind of resolve is needed. Put in for a transfer now before it is too late.

> As ever,
> Your oul' segocia,
> Mocky Fondoo.

> The Ivy Cottage,
> Lisnacoo,
> Ballyfee.

Dear Hamish,

To be a successful postman you need the patience of Job, the sagacity of Solomon and the perception of Plato. In addition you must be prepared to hear all, see all and say nothing. It is not easy to become a postman. You must have a knowledge of Irish. Only last week an auxiliary with twenty years experience who wanted to become a fulltime, pensionable postman was turned down because he could not name a single book written in Irish. Apparently he would have been appointed if he had known the name of such as *Twenty Years a-Growing* or *Jimín Mháire Thaidg.* Cavill the overseer was conducting the interview with a scholarly looking fellow from the head office.

'Have you any foreign language?' Cavill asked in the vain hope that he might still manage to salvage the job for the applicant.

'I have a smattering of massage parlour Swedish sir,' our man replied.

'By the six buttocks of the three musketeers,' said Cavil slapping his thigh, 'but that's a good answer, an imaginative answer.' The man from Dublin, however, was not impressed. Apparently regulations were regulations and a pretended knowledge of Irish was necessary.

'Say something to us in the native tongue,' Cavil begged in a last despairing effort.

'*Lá Breá,*' said our friend. This is Gaelic for a 'fine day' Hamish.

'I declare to God,' said Carvill, 'but he's made an accurate observation. It is a fine day.'

'*Lá breá,*' our friend repeated himself.

'By the twelve tits of the Vestal Virgins but that's fair comment,' Cavill said. The man from Dublin shook his head indicating that the interview was over. I myself became a postman the hard way. I passed the civil service examination at the age of fourteen after a long session of special coaching by my teachers. I spent four years as a telegram boy before I was allowed to lay hands on my first letter. I learned all the tricks for survival but I never had to use any. I was good at my job and I liked my job.

In my telegram days the Bugler McNulty was ticked off regularly for later deliveries or for arriving back at the office hours behind time. His argument was that he had too many calls when in point of fact he had too few. Always on his return he reeked with the smell of intoxicating drink.

46

One morning he found an overseer waiting for him. This was a taciturn martinet of a fellow from the Limerick office. The overseer was astonished at the end of the day to find that the Bugler had been telling the truth. But how had he managed to dupe this expert? Over the preceding months he had been collecting windows — i.e. bills which had been posted by local merchants to debtors along his route. The Bugler dare not do this with normal mail but nobody wants a bill so he was quite safe. On the morning in question the overseer sprung himself upon the Bugler out of the blue. From the moment he received his bag the overseer fastened himself to the Bugler's side. The collected bills were hidden behind some wainscotting in the sorting office. The problem was how to get at them without being spotted by the overseer. As they were leaving the office the Bugler turned to one of the clerks at the counter and in a very refined accent addressed him:

'Like a good chap,' said the Bugler, 'would you mind fetching my lunch from the sorting office?'

There was a general titter at this both from the customers and the clerks. Wasn't it well known that the Bugler's sole means of sustenance was porter. The clerk, however, sensed that the Bugler was in trouble.

'Where is it?' he asked while the overseer fumed at the doorway.

'In the wall pantry,' the Bugler informed him. Then in a whisper he revealed that it was behind the wainscotting. The clerk disappeared and returned at once with the parcel. It was covered with cobwebs but the Bugler fobbed it inside his bag before the overseer could catch a glimpse of it. Outside the door the Bugler mounted his bicycle and the overseer mounted his. When they left the village the Bugler dismounted and informed the overseer that he was going behind a ditch to answer a call of nature. In a matter of minutes the bills were mixed with the normal mail. It was late that night when the pair returned.

In less than a month I'll be delivering my last letter. I

don't know what I'll do apart from the fishing. The wife has sent word that she's staying in America until Christmas. The children need her. 'Tis lonely enough as it is. There is nothing else that is noteworthy. I'll close for the present. Regards to the wife.

As ever,
Your oul' segocia,
Mocky Fondoo.

P. S. The phone strike is still on and the longer it lasts the more precarious Katie Kersey's position becomes. The nun seldom comes now although it is widely known, in spite of their holiness, that some nuns have an insatiable appetite for news and chocolate.

Mocky.

Sarsfield Mews,
Upper Shoe Street,
Cork.

Dear Mocky,

How do you fight them off? There's a widow now does have a glass of hot whiskey ready for me if there's the slightest chill in the mornings. She sweetens it with sugar and flavours it with a slice of lemon and some cloves. It makes a nice start to the day. Rosanna was never better. We had a midnight swim recently in a stream about a mile or so from her home. What a night we had racing through the rushes and pelting water on top of one another. She's the gayest sod that was ever put into the world and there's no obligation of any kind after a night with her. What about those anonymous letters? Did they stop or did you find out the sender? Let me know all at your convenience. I have more women than I can cope with. I never believed it possible. My wildest dreams have come true and it's all due to the uniform.

Sincerely,
Frank O'Looney.

Dear Mocky,

Please don't think I'm taking advantage of you. This is positively the last time I'll bother you. Could you bring the usual items with you and I'll fix up with you at the end of the month.

Kitty.

The Ivy Cottage,
Lisnacoo,
Ballyfee.

Dear Frank,

As the tree falls so shall it lie or if you want it another way those who live by the sword shall perish by the sword or maybe you think you're blessed with a special immunity. No man with his possessions intact who behaves as you do can escape his destiny. No doubt, however, you'll keep making hay while the sun shines. At least you'll have the memory when the storm clouds appear. About the writer of the anonymous letters I have a happy tale to tell. We nailed him, Dogmeat Monsell and myself but we spent many a miserable night before we succeeded. No doubt you'll unknowingly deliver many an anonymous letter. You can take it from me that you'll never deliver a greater evil to the innocent persons who are at the receiving end. The chief cause underlying the writing of these dreadful epistles is jealousy. There is no other reason. The writers are consumed with it so that it becomes an illness from which there is no reprieve. Dogmeat and I suspected the same man. His name: Jonsy Josey McDill from Sradbally Lower. He lives with his mother and sells pool coupons, Sweep Tickets, etcetera for a living. What made me suspect him in the first place was a chance remarked dropped by a woman of my acquaintance whose husband is in England. She is a Mrs Norris, Kitty to be more precise. Jonsy Josey chanced his arm with her several times and in the end became so amorous that she was forced to bar him from the house. I had nothing else to go on. Dogmeat Monsell on the other hand had his own way of discovering the scoundrel. When I first told him that Kitty Norris and I had been receiving anonymous letters in the taproom of the 'Lisnacoo Elms' as we were enjoying a few pints together one night he concluded immediately that Jonsy Josey McDill was the man. When I asked him for proof he said he needed none.

'He looks like a writer of anonymous letters,' said Dogmeat. 'Under that calm exterior lurks a slimy merchant. Have no doubt. He's the man.' Dogmeat wasn't surprised when I told him of the incidents with Kitty. Suspicions, however, were of little use unless we could catch him red-handed. There was always the distinct possibility that we could be completely wrong. We had no clues at the beginning but then they began to appear and a pattern that was to solve all our problems began to emerge. The first anonymous letter which Kitty Norris received was posted the night before. On this night occurred a very severe rainstorm. The second letter received by Kitty was posted the night before as well. On that night there was a fierce gale blowing and you wouldn't put a dog out of doors. The letter I received was posted the night before and was still damp when I located it in the post office that morning. It had been raining heavily the night before. Here at last was a pointer. Whoever the writer was he or she only posted a letter upon a particularly bad night and with good reason. You won't find many people abroad on wet and stormy nights. The chances of meeting anybody are slender in the extreme. An ideal time, therefore, for dirty work.

Each wet or stormy night afterwards Dogmeat would park his van outside the post office front door. The front faced on to the roadway and the back, which was provided with a door, as close as possible to the letter box. With a dozen of stout between us and a dart of poitcheen now and then we would sit in the rear of the van. Any person coming

or going the road would see that the vehicle was empty at
first appearances. There was no way of knowing that we sat
behind the front seats swigging away at our porter bottles
and conversing in whispers. At the least sound from the
roadway we dried up altogether and held our breaths. Then
on the fourth night which happened to be squally, wet and
unfit for travel we heard the sound of muffled footsteps on
the roadway. As they came closer we lay flat on our backs
in case our visitor should decide to peep in through the
windscreen. Several times we heard the light footfalls circling
the van. Then they stoppped and the vital moment was at
hand. My heart thumped in my breast like a drum and my
breathing became so strained that I feared it must give me
away. Then we heard a rustling movement as if a cape or
raincoat were being loosened or tightened. Of one accord
we burst through the backdoors of the van. There stood
Jonsy Josey McDill with a letter in his hand.

Upon seeing us he let out a terrible screech the likes of
which would remind you of nothing but the death squeal of
a stuck pig. Before we could lay hands on him he took to
his heels with Dogmeat and myself in hot pursuit. As he
fled along the roadway he tore pieces from the letter and
flung them into the air. We nailed him on the outskirts of
the village just as he was about to take off across country.
But for a despairing dive by Dogmeat the scoundrel might
have escaped our clutches. We confiscated the remains of
the letter and collected the pieces as we retraced our footsteps. In the kitchen of my own cottage we sat him near the
fire and pieced the letter together. It was addressed to Kitty
Norris and it contained page after page of the most heinous
obscenities. He cringed and whined and trembled by the
fire but neither Dogmeat nor myself could find it in our
hearts to feel pity for him. He begged for mercy and
explained that no door would be opened to him if word of
what he had done spread throughout the countryside. He
was particularly vulnerable, he explained, because of the
type of work in which he was engaged. As he sat there

whimpering, Dogmeat and I held a whispered council and after a while came to what we considered to be the most sensible solution. Jonsy Josey was to pay one hundred pounds forthwith to Kitty Norris. He was never again to write another anonymous letter and he was to pay a daily fifteen minutes visit to the parish church asking God's forgiveness. This was to be the price of silence until we decided to review his case again in the not-too-distant future. For good measure we assisted him to the bounds of the village with several well-aimed kicks in the arse. He handed me the money the following day and in turn I handed it over to Kitty. It was a Godsend to her. The husband sends her nothing whatsoever.

I myself am of the belief that people who write anonymous letters are in need of psychiatric treatment and also perhaps they need more understanding and compassion than we are prepared to give them. However there can be no disputing the fact that it is the most foul resort to which a man can turn in order to vent his spleen on his fellow human beings. I'll say no more for now except to warn you that unless you avoid the McDoogle traphouse you will get your fingers burnt.

As ever,
Your oul' segocia,
Mocky Fondoo.

P. S. Another likely way out of your predicament is to involve yourself with as many women as you can at this present time. There is safety in numbers.

Mocky.

Templebawn,
Ballyfee.

Dear Mister Fondoo,

I hesitates ere I writes to you. There was a parcel posted to me lately by my sister Nancy in London. When I went to enquire to the head office they told me the parcel's con-

52

tents was exposed and that they were destroyed according to the law. Now Mister Fondoo what would they want with confiscating fingerstalls? Fingerstalls is what is known as medical objects. There is another parcel coming soon, better wrapped with the same commodities inside and I implore of you to see that they gets delivered. My poor husband has very sore fingers as might get festered easy if not wrapped with care.

Your sincere friend,
Catríona Cooney (Mrs).

Wangle Avenue,
Off Sidberry Row,
Glasgow.

Dear Mocky,

I have a few days leave coming up and I am at a loss to know what to do with it. The missus wants to go to London to do a spot of shopping. Then there's my brother Angus in Kilmarnock I haven't seen for years. If I go to London I'll buy you something suitable to mark your retirement. I'm sorry for Kitty Norris and I have an idea what it must be like for her but don't you think my old friend that the answer to her problems lies in her own hands. Far be it from me to offer a man of your background and experience unwanted advice. However I feel that in view of our long friendship I have earned that right. Here in Glasgow there are thousands of Kitty Norris's. They seem to manage quite well after a while. There are state aids and other agencies to help them as I'm sure there must be in your country and I think Kitty would be well advised to get in touch without delay with one of these. The least that would happen is that there would be an easing of her financial worries. There are generous allowances for deserted wives. What I'm trying to say Mocky is that you and I, in spite of our ages, are maybe fools at heart and more susceptible than most to the plight of a lovely woman like Kitty. I am not suggesting for a moment that you are enamoured of her or have been smitten with one of those latter-day obsessions so common to fellows of our age. What I'm saying is that you might be over-concerned and as a result might become more involved than is wise. I speak from experience. Just bear in mind that there is a limit to what you can do for her, that you are restricted by other commitments. Oh dammit all Mocky my real worry is that you might make a fool of yourself. I hope I haven't said too much. A few years ago I became over-protective towards a girl in the office after her father died. I should have known better. I made a fool of myself. It's so bloody easy to make a fool of oneself when there's a young woman involved.

Write soon and let me know the details of your retirement and all the other odds and ends of news concerning Lisnacoo and Ballyfee. I'm tired out at the moment so I'll conclude.

Yours sincere friend,
Hamish MacShamus.

Sradbally Lower,
Ballyfee.

Dear Mocky Fondoo,

My letter to that lovely decent man, the Knight of Malta has been returned to me marked address unknown. They don't know much that don't know where Malta is.

Nance Nolan.

The Ivy Cottage,
Lisnacoo,
Ballyfee.

Dear Bridget,

I hope you're having a great time. The weather is fine here and from everywhere these days comes the sound of mowing machines as the meadows begin to fall in the hills and valleys. I would have written sooner but I have been up till all hours of late and the sleep is playing hell with me. There is the devil to pay here. The office was visited today by the postmaster, two overseers and the local Civic Guard who has been holding a sort of watching brief. I was questioned closely myself until Mr Mallvey stepped in and announced that I was above suspicion. Katey refused to answer any of the questions put to her and pretended she knew nothing about anything. The real cause of all the rumpus was the mixing up of two envelopes, almost impossible to distinguish from each other because of a similarity in size and bulk. What happened is this:

One of the letters was addressed to Father Kimmerley the parish priest while the other was intended for Catríona Cooney of Templebawn. Father Kimmerley's letter contained samples of cardboard and plastic Saint Patrick's Day badges manufactured by local nuns. His Lordship the Bishop had misgivings about the quality of the badges and because Kimmerley has a reputation in artistic matters the bishop wanted his opinion before making any decision concerning them. The letter which was addressed to Catríona Cooney contained five plastic packets of contraceptives. By some mysterious means, well known to all who know Katie Kersey, the Saint Patrick's Day badges wound up in Catríona Cooney's envelope while the contraceptives ended in Father Kimmerley's. With the contraceptives was a short note from his Lordship:

'Let me know,' it said, 'what you think of these. If you approve I'll give the nuns a free hand in their manufacture.' With the badges was an equally short note from Catríona's sister:

'One day,' it read, 'I hope these will be for sale publicly in Ireland.'

I don't know what the eventual outcome of this wretched mix-up will be. Katie seems to be wearing up well although there is a tenseness barely visible for all her outward calm. She has no one to fall back on. The nun has made no appearance since the trouble started. No blame to her. She dare not involve herself in any sort of scandal. Katie has never been very communicative. She has always resolutely depended on herself and herself alone. Of course they really are wasting their time asking questions. The combined forces of the Gestapo and the N.K.V.D. wouldn't knock a single tittle out of Katie Kersey. I must say, however, that this is the most serious business yet.

There is no more to report except that I miss you every day and night and long more than anything else in the world to have you back home again. Not to worry too much about the children. Things will sort themselves out. Everything works itself out in due course. Give them my love and let me assure you and them that all of you are constantly in my prayers.

Your loving husband,
Mocky.

Templebawn,
Ballyfee.

Dear Mocky,

I hesitates ere I writes to you. All's well as ends well as the lady said what thought she was expecting and was not. Father Kimmerley landed here. I'd have run in hide if I seen him in time. The man is a saint and 'tis well I knows his views on certain matters but he spoke out whatever. Says he what's your is your and what's mine is mine Catríona. We made our exchange and he bade me God bless. All's well as ends well.

Yours sincere friend,
Catríona Cooney.

Cahircoddle Heights,
Cahircoddle Upper,
Cork.

Mr and Mrs Percy McDoogle,
request the pleasure of the company of
Mocky and Bridget
on the occasion of the marriage of their daughter
Rosanna
to
Mr Frank O'Looney
in Saint Mary's Church, Cahircoddle,
on
Friday, July 31st
at 2 o'clock
and afterwards at the reception in
The Silver Birch Hotel,
Cork.

R.S.V.P.

The Ivy Cottage,
Lisnacoo,
Ballyfee.

Dear Hamish,

I appreciate the sentiments expressed in your letter and take no exception whatsoever. You always had an uncanny knack of hitting the nail upon the head. Kitty Norris has gone. There's a FOR SALE on one of the windows of the house and rumour has it that she left in an attempt to rejoin Jack in England. She must have located him because I understand that the house was in their joint names. I remember the day it first dawned on her that he was two-timing. It was I who delivered the letter just a few months ago. It was written by a school friend of Kitty's to whom she had written requesting information about Jack. The friend was blunt. Jack was shacked up with a divorcee who also happened to run a boarding house. He has stopped sending money. His wife and children might have starved but for me. That's another matter altogether, however, and I don't expect any kudos for that.

I remember that letter well. I knew by the handwriting it was from a woman and the postmark told me that it was dispatched from the same postal district from which used arrive Jack's registered letters. Kitty asked me to wait while she read it. This is common enough along the route. The letter might require an immediate answer and only a churlish postman would not respond. When she finished she laid the letter on the table. Tears appeared in her eyes. It was a bitter blow. Certainly she had given Jack no cause to be unfaithful. She had, in fact, been a model wife and no one but a restless and discontented wretch would consider leaving her. She laid a hand on the table and fought to keep back the tears. I'm sure she must have asked herself why her beauty and fidelity had been so heedlessly spurned by the only man to whom she had ever given herself. A woman will never fully recover from a blow like this. The tragedy of her situation was reflected in her face. The next thing was that I found her in my arms. For a long time she sobbed out her sorrow. There was no way I could alleviate her misery except to wait until the last tear had fallen.

I held her in my arms for as long as she wanted to be held and released her the moment she wished to be released. I'll never forget the warmth of her tears on my face or the soft tender touch of her dark hair as it whispered unholy thoughts to my overworked heart. Foolish old man you will say but a man can be old and not be blind to beauty in distress. Age may do a lot of things but it does not make a man insensitive. All it can do is make him old. Now that she's gone I know how old I really am. I had come to look forward to bringing her groceries from Lisnacoo and if there were times when she hadn't the money her wants made no great inroads into my reserves.

I cannot say that what I felt for her was completely lacking in carnality but I think I can say that my own loneliness because of Bridget's absence and her undeniable beauty were factors that made my visits to her the most exciting prospects of these lonesome days.

As you said in your letter the answer to her problem was in her own hands all the time. The simple and natural solution was to follow her mate. After all she had taken him on for better or for worse and then there were the children. Not all women would go after him. I'm glad she didn't tell me beforehand that she intended leaving. It was characteristic of her to leave with the minimum of fuss. To be honest Hamish I'll miss her, not the way I miss my wife but the way I'd miss a memorable landmark such as a favourite stretch of water or the brow of a hill lighted by the red rays of a declining sun. There's more to it of course than just that. I have no doubt you understand. There is an ache for which there is no immediate cure. Enough of this foolishness. These are luxuries beyond a man of my years and on top of that the show must go on. For the present then I'll sign off. Regards to the missus. I hope you enjoy your few days off.

As ever,
Your oul' segocia,
Mocky Fondoo.

Sarsfield Mews,
Upper Shoe Street,
Cork.

Dear Mocky,

Don't say it. Don't say I told you so. By this time you will have received the invitation from Percy and Mrs McDoogle. The uniform has turned out to be the rope that finally hung me although that's harsh because Rosanna is a fine girl and will make a splendid wife. You were right when you said I wouldn't wear out my first pair of pants before joining the ranks of the martyrs. It must be an all-time record for a postman, three months on the job and already engaged to be married.

Now I have a very special request. Could you see your way towards being my best man? There is nobody I'd rather have. You would want to let me know by return as the moment of truth is at hand. The reason for the early date is that Rosanna will be due about six months after and the McDoogle's don't want to give the neighbours anything to say. I've only known her three months which may not seem like a long time but by the hokey I saw more action in that space of time than most men see in a lifetime. The baby will be a premature one to the tune of three months so suspicion is bound to be aroused. However, as you so often said yourself people only addle themselves with suspicion. I wish you luck and joy on the occasion of your retirement. You were a man I always looked up to when I was a gorsoon down there and I could see from the way the people looked at you and spoke to you that you were highly regarded in your district. You were a bit proud maybe and you often refused a good dinner when you shouldn't have but, by God, none of those people would ever dream of putting a hard word on you.

Don't delay in answering this. I can get plenty to stand up for me around here but you're the man I want whatever is in you. Rosanna sends her love and we both look forward to having you at our wedding.

Sincerely,
Frank O'Looney.

P. S. That widow I told you about who makes the hot whiskey for me keeps lodgers now and then. I'll book you in there for the night as soon as you let me know you're coming.

Frank.

The Ivy Cottage,
Lisnacoo,
Ballyfee.

Dear Frank,

Congratulations on your engagement. Let me assure you that you have broken no records. Dogmeat Monsell delivered his first letter to a young widow by the name of Katie-Go-Down of a Tuesday morning in May close on thirty years ago and on the following Saturday the pair were spotted in the city of Limerick where they went to purchase an engagement ring. That amounts to five days. They were married the following Saturday which amounts to twelve days. Now that's a record for you. Her real name was Kate McKenna but she was nicknamed Go-Down after her father Micky-Go-Down who used the expression 'go down damn you' to chastise his dogs or to disagree with humans. They live happily Dogmeat and Katie and as soon as I retire in a week's time it is almost certain that Dogmeat's son Martin will step into my shoes. He's qualified for the job.

I'll gladly be your best man although I believe you should have asked some friend of yours nearer your own age. Still I'm honoured and flattered. Katie Kersey was carried away yesterday on the nun's instructions. Katie hasn't been herself for some time. Three days ago she was suspended from her position as postmistress after the biggest mix-up in the history of the post office. In the end nobody was receiving the right letters but believe it or not there is talk of submitting a petition to the minister to have her reinstated.

The night before she was taken away she attempted to say mass in the phone booth which stands outside the P. O. She read the Gospel from the telephone directory starting at random with the word Jordanian and ending quite solemnly but quite accidentally with the phrase *Jubilate Deo* from the famous canticle of the same name. She looked like a high priestess in her long nightgown. It transpired later from what could be made of her sermon that she was praying for forgiveness for the souls of Lisnacoo and Ballyfee. In the middle of the ceremony Father Kimmerley arrived and led her indoors quietly. Doctor Mongie was summoned and she was put under sedation. I understand she's quite happy in her place of confinement. She spends the day reading invisible letters and seems to knock great enjoyment out of it. You might say she's chewing the cud. Dick Cavill has taken over the running of the post office until somebody new is appointed.

'By the twenty breast nipples of Niall and the Nine Hostages,' said he, 'but this is the greatest mess since Moses came down from the mountain.'

There's little else of interest. In view of the fact that the wife is in the States I presume it will be alright if I bring Dogmeat Monsell along to the wedding. He has a car and in addition he might be a better candidate for your widow's favours. See you soon then.

As ever,
Your oul' segocia,
Mocky Fondoo.

The Ivy Cottage,
Lisnacoo.

My dear Bridget,

Well it has happened at last although I can still feel the strap of the bag across my shoulders. The Bugler McNulty once told me that it never really goes away. As I write this the hammers of hell are pounding in my head. When I handed in my bag for the last time last evening Dick Cavill suggested we make for the 'Lisnacoo Elms' for a farewell drink and to discuss arrangements for the presentation and dinner which is to be held on my behalf later in the year in some hotel in town. We went into the back lounge where a huge bright bouquet of summer blooms greeted us from the open hearth. Dick called for two whiskies and while we sat there reminiscing I felt a great loneliness inside me. The tears came to my eyes. I think Dick understood for he placed a hand upon my shoulder and said in a low voice: 'Fifty years is a long time. By the eight kidneys of the Four Horsemen of the Apocalypse,' said he, 'but it's a long time old son.' Then one by one all the gang started to drift in until soon every postman in the district was present. The postmaster came and so did the clerks and soon the beer flowed. At the height of our sing-song the door opened and who should appear in his tweeds and old grey beard but Hamish MacShamus. Very soon he was as drunk as the rest of us and we lifted the roof with the chorus of *Loch Lomond*. I do not remember going home to the cottage. All I remember is being awakened an hour ago by Hamish who handed me a mug of tea and informed me that the water in the river was dropping fast and it would be fit for fishing in less than two hours. It's a strange feeling that's on me since I woke. I doubt if I'll ever really get used to it. There's a guilt in me that shouldn't be there and it's as if the people I served for so long were beckoning me to get on with the job. Even if I wanted I can't do that now.

There were many other well-wishers who sent cards and letters and the letters weren't without their tokens of appreciation. There was also a parcel which contained one of the loveliest fishing spools I ever saw. The sender was anonymous, somebody in England. It could be one of a thousand. I won't tell you how much I miss you but it will be a long summer and a longer autumn without you. For a while then my love I'll bid you adieu.

Your loving husband,
Mocky.

*   *   *